THE REAL MADRID ANNUAL 2017

Written by Iain Spragg

CONTENTS

Welcome to the Real Madrid Annual 2017, essential reading for fans of the record-breaking Spanish giants.

The most successful team in the history of Spanish football after winning more league and European titles than any of their rivals, Real Madrid added further silverware to their amazing trophy cabinet in 2016 after winning the Champions League in Milan.

Victory gave Los Blancos an incredible 11th European crown, four more than any other club.

With global stars Cristiano Ronaldo, Gareth Bale and Karim Benzema, Madrid is a team which is famous across the world. And in manager Zinedine Zidane they have one of the few men in football who has won the European Cup, European Championship and the World Cup as a player.

The Real Madrid Annual 2017 has everything you need to know about the club – from the lowdown on the squad and the Bernabeu stadium in numbers to the ten greatest goals the side scored during the 2015-16 season.

All you have to do is sit back and enjoy!

ANO 2016

REAL RULE EUROPE

The most successful side in the history of European club football, Los Blancos lifted the Champions League trophy for a record-breaking 11th time in 2016 after beating city rivals Atletico Madrid in a dramatic final in Italy.

No team has been crowned the Champions of Europe more times than Real Madrid. The Spanish giants won their 10th title in 2014 after thrashing Atletico Madrid 4-1 and they pulled off another famous victory over their neighbours two years later to take the Champions League trophy back to the Bernabeu.

More than 70,000 fans packed into the San Siro stadium in Milan to watch the final and although Atletico took the game into extra-time and then penalties, Los Blancos were on target with all five shots from the spot in the shootout.

Top scorer Cristiano Ronaldo was the match winner, scoring with the crucial fifth penalty, and Madrid were officially the best team in Europe once again.

Los Blancos began their Champions League campaign in brilliant form with a 4-0 demolition of Shakhtar Donetsk at the Bernabeu in September, Ronaldo registering a hat-trick to get the side off to a flyer in Group A.

They beat Swedish side Malmo 2-0 two weeks later and although they were held to a goalless draw by PSG in October, they beat the French champions in the return fixture in Spain thanks to a goal from substitute Nacho. It was a result which confirmed the team's place in the Last 16 with two games to spare.

Goals from Ronaldo (2), Luka Modric and Dani Carvajal earned Los Blancos a 4-3 win over Shakhtar in Ukraine and they finished off the group in style in December, demolishing Malmo 8-0 at the Bernabeu. Ronaldo scored four and Karim Benzema notched a hat-trick as the side equalled the record for the biggest-ever victory in the history of the Champions League.

Madrid swapped managers in January when Zinedine Zidane took over from Rafa Benitez but the change in the dugout made no difference to the side's dazzling performances in Europe as they marched through to the final.

Italian
team
Roma were
the opposition in
the Last 16 in February
but the fixture was over
as a contest after the first leg.
Ronaldo and Jesé got the goals in
the Stadio Olimpico to give the side a
2-0 advantage and they wrapped up their
place in the next round with another 2-0 win
in Madrid three weeks later.

Los Blancos received a big shock in the first
leg of their quarter-final against Wolfsburg,
losing 2-0 in Germany, but Ronaldo came to
the rescue in the second leg in Spain with an
incredible hat-trick which kept the dream of
Champions League glory alive.

REAL RULE EUROPE

Real were through to the semi-finals. They were drawn against Manchester City but the loss of Ronaldo to a thigh injury and two brilliant later saves from goalkeeper Joe Hart in the first leg at the Etihad saw the match finish goalless.

Ronaldo was back for the second leg at the Bernabeu but it was Gareth Bale who did the damage in Spain, his fierce shot deflecting off City midfielder Fernando in the first-half for the only goal of the match.

At the end of May Los Blancos headed to Italy for the final and the clash with Atletico. Los Blancos hadn't won in either of their two La Liga fixtures against their city rivals earlier in the season but found a way to beat Diego Simeone's side when it mattered most.

REAL RULE EUROPE

Los Blancos struck first in the San Siro. Germany midfielder Toni Kroos delivered a 15th minute free kick into the box, Bale rose above Atletico defenders to brilliantly flick it on with his head and captain Sergio Ramos was in the right place to steer the ball into the back of the net from close range.

Ramos had been on target for Madrid in the final in 2014 and his opener in Milan meant he became the first defender in the history of the competition to score in two different Champions League finals.

Atletico forward Antoine Griezmann missed the chance to equalise early in the second-half when he smashed his penalty against the crossbar but they did score 11 minutes before full-time when substitute Yannick Carrasco netted and just like in 2014, the final went into extra-time.

Real had scored three times in the additional 30 minutes two years earlier but there were no more goals this time in the San Siro and the winners would have to be decided by a penalty shootout.

Lucas Vazquez, Marcelo, Bale and Ramos were all on target from the spot with the first four Madrid penalties. Juanfran missed Atletico's fourth effort and it was left to Ronaldo to step forward and clinch the cup after sending the goalkeeper the wrong way.

"I had the feeling I would score the winning goal," Ronaldo said. "I told Zidane to leave me to last and it went well. Winning my third Champions League title is a dream. We are really happy because finals are always hard. The team were great and sacrificed a lot for this. There are no words to describe the happiness that we feel. It's a special moment." (uefa.com)

Victory for Los Blancos gave Zidane his first trophy as the Madrid manager, just five months after getting the Bernabeu job. The Frenchman became only the second man to win the Champions League with Real as a player and then as the club's manager.

"At the end getting the Champions League is the best along with winning the World Cup," Zidane said after the final. "After all the work we did I am very proud, it has been a phenomenal job. I'm happy because I've been part of this great club for a long time now."

"You always have to dream, think positive, be optimistic, and know that things can get done with work and effort. I'm very happy for everything we've achieved together. It's not easy at all. We've really worked hard, fought it out. When you have players of this calibre, with this talent, you can achieve something big like we have tonight." (skysports.com)

Ramos lifted the trophy in what was his first season as the club captain and was also named the Man of the Match in Milan.

"This is a wonderful feeling," he said. "It's a real reward for us after a hard season. We got to this final and winning it again, it's incredible. The emotion is unforgettable. It will always have a very special place in my heart.

"Atletico played very well, they've had a great season, but the nature of football is that both teams can't win and fortunately the cup is coming home with us. To hold that cup in my hands as part of the best team in the world, in my first year as captain, is amazing." (uefa.com)

LA LIGA

ONE OF THE MOST EXCITING TITLE RACES FOR YEARS, Los Blancos battled with both Barcelona and Atletico Madrid all season to be crowned champions in Spain. It went down to the wire and in the last round of matches, Los Blancos missed out on a record 33rd title by just one point.

Madrid were looking for their first La Liga triumph in four years and they started the season with a bang, winning five of their first six games to go top of the table. The run included a 5-0 thrashing of Real Betis and a 6-0 victory over Espanyol and by the end of September the team was out in front.

2015-16 REVIEW

The start of the side's Champions League challenge, however, saw a dip in form in the league, suffering back-to-back defeats in November which saw Los Blancos surrender the top spot. A 3-2 loss away to Seville was followed by defeat at the Bernabeu against Barcelona in El Clasico and Rafa Benitez's side was playing catch-up.

The team won four of their next five league games to keep the pressure on the leaders Barcelona, but in early January they were held to a 2-2 draw by Valencia at the Mestalla Stadium and the next day the club parted ways with Benitez.

On the same day, Madrid announced that Zinedine Zidane, the club's second team manager, had been promoted to replace Benitez and, under the Frenchman, the side only lost one more La Liga fixture that season.

"I want to thank the club and thank the president for giving me the opportunity to train this club," the new boss said. "It's the best club in the world with the best fan base in the world. I want to do my very best to ensure that this club at the end of the season will have a trophy." (bbc.co.uk)

" I WANT TO THANK THE CLUB AND THANK THE PRESIDENT FOR GIVING ME THE OPPORTUNITY TO TRAIN THIS CLUB. "

His first game in charge was against Deportivo La Coruna at the Bernabeu and the players responded to their new manager brilliantly, Gareth Bale hitting a fantastic hat-trick as Los Blancos beat the visitors 5-0.

Eight days later they hit five again as they mauled Sporting Gijon 5-1 in Madrid but the highlight of Zidane's short stint as the new boss came in early April when his team headed to the Nou Camp for the second El Clasico of the season.

Los Blancos were desperate for revenge after losing to their arch-rivals at the Bernabeu and they got it with a dramatic 2-1 victory. The home side scored first but Madrid fought back and equalised with an amazing scissor kick from Karim Benzema after 62 minutes.

A red card for captain Sergio Ramos late on reduced Los Blancos to 10 men but there was still time for Cristiano Ronaldo to grab the winner, the Portuguese superstar chesting down Bale's excellent cross before he nutmegged the goalkeeper with a fierce shot.

"We know we can beat anyone on our day," Bale said after the match. "Everyone says that Barcelona are the best team but we have beaten them in their own backyard, so mentally it puts us in a great position. There is a long way to go in the league and Champions League and we just need to keep going." (walesonline.co.uk)

The result was part of an incredible 11-match winning run by Real through March, April and May which kept the team firmly in the hunt for silverware and they prepared for the final game of the season against Deportivo La Coruna at the Estadio Riazor within touching distance of Barcelona.

LA LIGA
2015-16 REVIEW

Los Blancos were just one point behind the defending champions and knew that if they beat Deportivo and the Catalans lost against Granada that Zidane's team would win La Liga.

Madrid took all three points on the road against Deportivo, two goals from Ronaldo in the first half doing the damage to steer the side to a remarkable 12th successive win. But it was heartbreak for Los Blancos when they heard news that Barcelona had won 3-0 against Granada and were the champions.

Real had finished the season in great style but it was not quite enough to lift the trophy.

"We're a little disappointed after the effort we made," Zidane said. "After 38 league games we can't change the fact Barcelona are champions. They deserved to win the league but I take my hat off to my lads. We might have had difficult moments but we never gave up and we kept fighting to the end. I'm very proud of everyone in this team, all I can do is give them encouragement." (reuters.com)

THE KING OF

CRISTIANO RONALDO'S SEVENTH SEASON WITH REAL MADRID was another sensational one as the Portuguese superstar steered Los Blancos to Champions League glory and rewrote the record books to become the club's all-time leading goalscorer.

It was only a matter of time before Ronaldo became the greatest-ever striker in the history of the Spanish giants. He has been an unstoppable goal machine ever since his world record £80million move from Manchester United back in 2009 and 2015-16 was the season in which he was officially crowned Madrid's top scorer.

His first record-breaking feat came in September when the Portuguese genius smashed five past Espanyol in the league. This incredible achievement took his career haul in La Liga to 230 in only 227 appearances and in the process he overtook Raul's club record of 228 league goals.

Ronaldo was not finished there though and later the same month he was on target again against Swedish side Malmo in the group stages of the Champions League. The first of his two goals that night took him to an amazing 500 for club and country in his career.

In October the forward made more history when he grabbed one of Los Blancos's goals in a

THE BERNABEU

3-0 win over Levante at the Bernabeu. His strike was his 324th goal in the club's famous white shirt and once again he went ahead of Raul in the Madrid scoring charts, this time beating his old milestone for goals in all competitions.

It wasn't just Raul's records that Ronaldo smashed during his unbelievable season. A dazzling hat-trick in the Champions League against Shakhtar Donetsk in September saw him become the competition's all-time top scorer on 80 goals. He also netted a total of 11 times in Europe before Christmas to become the first-ever player to reach double figures in the group stages of the tournament.

Surprisingly, the star wasn't on target in the Champions League final itself but his 16 goals in only 12 games in Europe saw him finish as the competition's top scorer for a fourth year in a row.

No other player has been so deadly in the Champions League for so long.

The end of his net-busting campaign in May saw Ronaldo score twice in La Liga against Deportivo La Coruna. It took him to 51 goals in just 48 games for Los Blancos and was the sixth season running he had gone past the half century mark in front of goal. He is the first player in the history of football to have achieved that.

RONALDO

THE PORTUGUESE MAGICIAN HAS RIPPED UP THE RECORD BOOKS SINCE SIGNING FOR REAL MADRID. Here are some of the incredible scoring milestones the striker has set during his amazing Bernabeu career.

CHAMPIONS LEAGUE LEGEND

Ronaldo was on target 16 times in the Champions League in 2015-16 as Madrid were crowned champions, making him the competition's all-time top scorer with 94 goals in 131 games. He scored 16 for Manchester United, the other 78 coming in his seven seasons with Los Blancos.

HAT-TRICK HERO

No-one has scored more hat-tricks for Madrid than Ronaldo. His treble in the Champions League quarter-final second leg against Wolfsburg was the 37th of his remarkable career for the club. The star also jointly holds the record with Lionel Messi for the most Champions League hat-tricks with five. He registered three trebles in Europe in 2015-16, the first player ever to achieve the feat.

DOUBLE FINAL DELIGHT

Ronaldo is the only player to have hit the back of the net in the Champions League final for two different teams. He was on target for Manchester United against Chelsea in 2008 and then made history when he scored for Los Blancos against Atletico Madrid in 2014.

THE NEED FOR SPEED

The striker holds a series of La Liga records for quick-fire scoring. Ronaldo was the fastest player to reach both 150 and 200 league goals in Spain and in 2014-15 he was also the quickest ever man to register 20 league goals at the start of a season, setting the milestone after only 12 appearances.

SIX OF THE BEST

Ronaldo bagged 35 goals in 36 appearances in La Liga in 2015-16, making him the only player in the history of the Spanish league to score 30 or more in six seasons in a row.

KNOCKOUT KING

The Bernabeu star is deadly when it comes to the knockout stages of the Champions League. A total of 42 of his European goals have come after the group stages of the competition, making him the greatest-ever striker in the business end of the tournament. His incredible 17 goals in 2013-14 is also a Champions League record.

THE RECORD BREAKER

EL CLASICO LANDMARK

The Portuguese holds the record as the first player ever to score in six successive El Clasico games between Real Madrid and Barcelona. His amazing run began in the Copa del Rey in January 2012 and carried on until the two teams met in La Liga in October. The remarkable run brought seven goals in six appearances.

A SEASON TO REMEMBER

The 2014-15 campaign was one to remember for Ronaldo as he set two new scoring records for Los Blancos. His sensational 61-goal haul was the highest ever recorded by a Madrid player in a single season while his 48 strikes in La Liga was another new club milestone.

HIGH FIVE

Seven different players have scored five in a La Liga match for Madrid but Ronaldo is the only one to have done it twice. He hit five against Granada in April 2015 and he repeated the trick in September of the same year in a 6-0 demolition of Espanyol.

TOP 10

REAL MADRID HIT THE BACK OF THE NET AN AMAZING 141 TIMES IN JUST 52 MATCHES DURING THE 2015-16 SEASON. These are 10 of the best from the European champions.

GARETH BALE V REAL BETIS
The Welsh wizard collected the ball in enemy territory and surged towards goal. The defence desperately tried to close down the space only for the winger to unleash a stunning 40-yard effort with his left foot which swerved away from the keeper, hit the inside of the post and crashed in.

JAMES RODRIGUEZ V REAL BETIS
The second wonder goal from Los Blancos's 5-0 thrashing of Betis, Rodriguez's free kick was a stunner. The Colombian placed the ball on the right edge of the box and smashed it into the top far corner with a brilliant mix of power and bend.

NACHO V PSG
The defender only scored one goal in 2015-16 but it was a cracker. Gareth Bale's vicious shot was deflected high into the air and Nacho appeared from nowhere on the left to side foot volley the ball home against the French champions from an impossible angle.

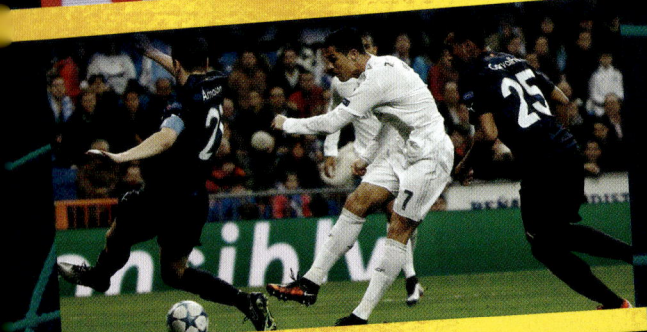

CRISTIANO RONALDO V MALMO
Los Blancos smashed eight past the Swedish team. Ronaldo grabbed four of them and the pick of the bunch was his unstoppable free kick from 35 yards at a wide angle. The Portuguese hit it hard and low and it rocketed into the bottom corner.

CRISTIANO RONALDO V REAL SOCIEDAD
Los Blancos's last match of 2015 saw their superstar score one of his trademark specials, getting to Marcelo's deep corner before the defence and then producing a beautiful volley from the edge of the box with his weaker left foot.

GOALS

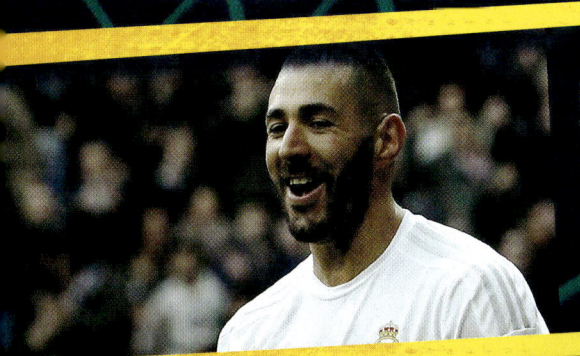

KARIM BENZEMA V SPORTING GIJON

The brilliant Frenchman grabbed 28 goals in 2015-16 and his most spectacular came in the 5-1 win over Gijon at the Bernabeu. Gareth Bale delivered the cross and Benzema put it away with a superb, horizontal bicycle kick which found the bottom left corner.

CRISTIANO RONALDO V ESPANYOL

This Ronaldo goal was all about his pace and skill as the Bernabeu star sprinted through a gap in the back four, left two defenders for dead with his tricks and then unleashed a fierce left-footed shot from the edge of the area which the keeper could do nothing to stop.

CRISTIANO RONALDO V ROMA

Los Blancos beat the Italians 4-0 on aggregate in their last 16 clash and Ronaldo got the ball rolling with the first of the four goals, beating the last defender with a stunning Cruyff turn to create the space for a sensational curler into the top corner.

LUKA MODRIC V VILLARREAL

Danilo's storming run down the right wing did the damage and his cross was perfect for Modric, the midfielder meeting the ball with a sliding left-footed volley which sailed into the back of the net.

GARETH BALE V MANCHESTER CITY

The goal that sent Madrid through to the Champions League final, Bale's winner at the Bernabeu was incredible. The Welsh hero seemed to have no time or space but still beat goalkeeper Joe Hart with his weaker right foot from a ridiculous angle.

CAPTAIN

THE DEFENSIVE ROCK AT THE HEART OF THE REAL MADRID BACK FOUR, SERGIO RAMOS ENJOYED A DREAM DEBUT SEASON AS THE NEW CLUB CAPTAIN IN 2015-16 AS HIS LOS BLANCOS SIDE PROUDLY LIFTED THE CHAMPIONS LEAGUE TROPHY.

When the news broke that veteran goalkeeper Iker Casillas was leaving the Bernabeu in the summer of 2015, Madrid found themselves looking for a new skipper. The search for Casillas's replacement was quick and it was Ramos who was handed the captain's armband.

The longest-serving member of the squad, the defender was of course the obvious choice. There had been speculation linking Ramos with a move to Manchester United but instead of quitting Spain for the Premier League, he accepted the captaincy and signed a new five-year deal with the club.

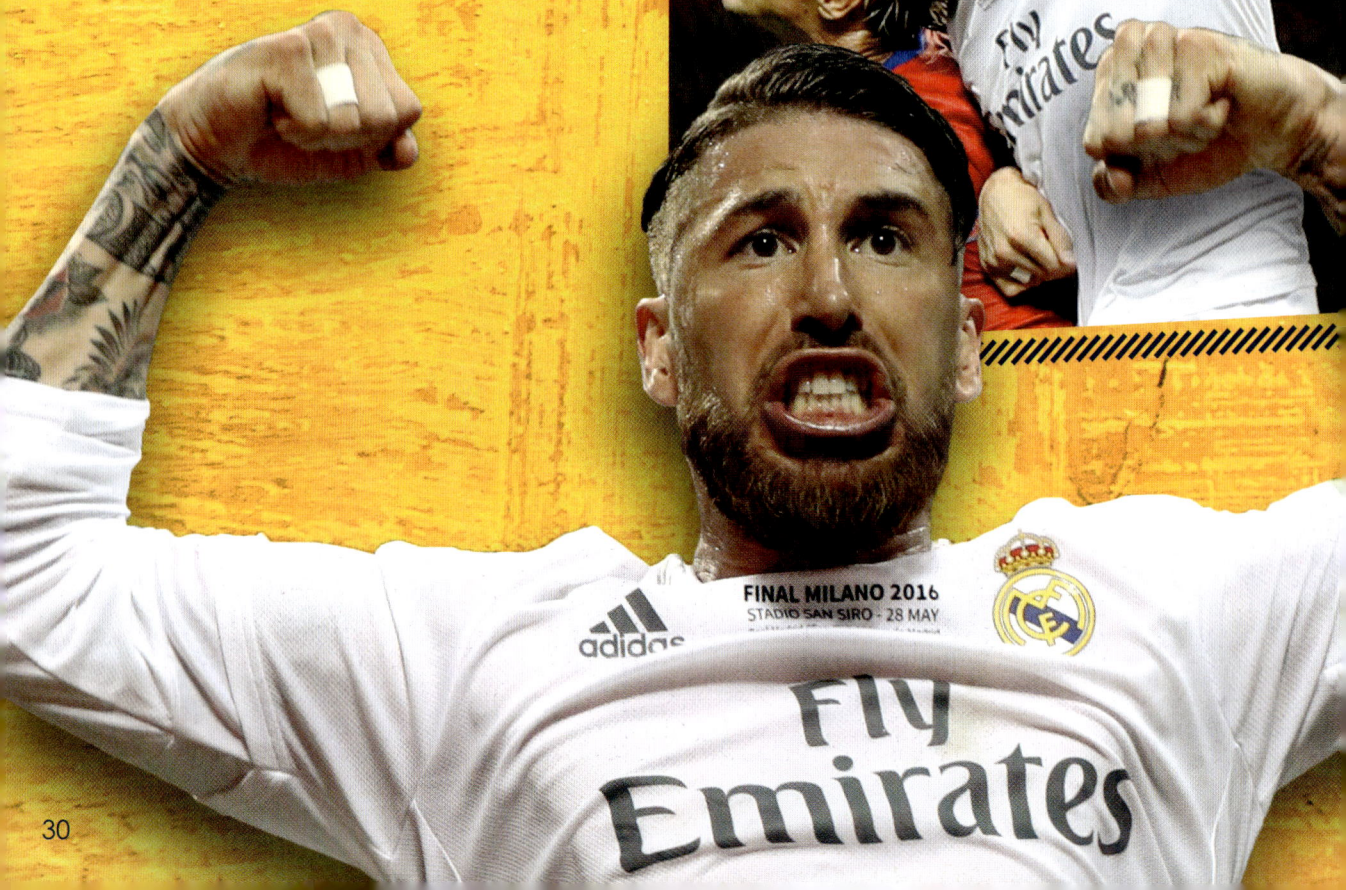

FANTASTIC

"My heart and head have always been with Real Madrid so I couldn't be happier," Ramos said after he was unveiled as the captain. "My idea was to always be here and I always wanted to retire here if the president would allow it. I'm thankful I have a new challenge to be the captain of this team. The priority is always Real Madrid, keeping our fans happy and winning titles." (skysports.com)

Less than a year after becoming the new leader of the team, Ramos made good on his promise of making the club's supporters happy when he led Los Blancos to glory in Europe as they beat arch-rivals Atletico in the final of the Champions League.

The centre back scored Madrid's only goal in the San Siro stadium in Milan and when the final went to a penalty shootout, the skipper had the courage to step up and score from the spot. Real won 5-4 and Ramos's brilliant captaincy had played a huge part in the club becoming European champions for a record 11th time.

Ramos began his professional career as a teenager with Seville in 2004. He spent only one season with the club but it was long enough to convince Madrid that the youngster was a star in the making and in the summer of 2005 Los Blancos paid £21.5million to bring him to the Bernabeu. It is still a record transfer fee in Spain for a teenager.

Despite having just one year of professional football behind him, Ramos immediately became a fixture in the first team and in his first season at Bernabeu he made 46 appearances in all competitions and scored six goals.

It was not long before he was claiming silverware with Los Blancos. He picked up his first winner's medal after Madrid won La Liga in 2006-07 and since that success, he has collected two more league titles as well as winning the Champions League twice, two Spanish Super Cups, the UEFA Super Cup and the FIFA Club World Cup in 2014.

One of his greatest moments in the club's famous white shirt came in 2014 in the Champions League final against Atletico Madrid, his brilliant second-half injury-time header in Lisbon dramatically sending the match into extra-time. Los Blancos had come within seconds of defeat but emerged 4-1 winners all thanks to Ramos's dramatic equaliser.

For a defender, the Real captain scores a remarkable number of goals. He has found the back of the net in all of his 11 seasons with the club and by the end of the 2015-16 campaign he had netted 58 times in 478 matches in all competitions.

His amazingly consistent performances have also seen Ramos claim many individual awards to go with his collection of winner's medals. He was named La Liga Breakthrough Player of the Year in 2005 and he has been voted La Liga's Best Defender four times. He was also named Man of the Match in the 2016 Champions League final and he has been included in the UEFA Team of the Year five times.

Ramos won his first cap for Spain while he was still a Seville player but his international career really took off after he arrived at the Bernabeu. He was part of the Spain team which won the European Championship in 2008 and then successfully defended their title four years later in Kiev. The Real star was also in the starting XI in South Africa in 2010 as Spain lifted the World Cup.

He joined an exclusive group of players in March 2013 when he won his 100th cap for his country in a World Cup qualifier against Finland and he now sits second on the all-time appearance list for Spain behind his former team-mate Casillas.

At club level, he is outside the top 10 for games for Madrid but having just signed a new contract that will keep him at the Bernabeu until 2020, he will soon surge past the 500-match mark and confirm his reputation as one of Los Blancos's greatest ever.

ROLL OF

REAL MADRID IS THE MOST SUCCESSFUL CLUB IN THE HISTORY OF SPANISH FOOTBALL. Here's a full rundown of Los Blancos's incredible collection of silverware and the players who've won individual awards during their Bernabeu careers.

LA LIGA (32)

1931–32, 1932–33, 1953–54, 1954–55, 1956–57, 1957–58, 1960–61, 1961–62, 1962–63, 1963–64, 1964–65, 1966–67, 1967–68, 1968–69, 1971–72, 1974–75, 1975–76, 1977–78, 1978–79, 1979–80, 1985–86, 1986–87, 1987–88, 1988–89, 1989–90, 1994–95, 1996–97, 2000–01, 2002–03, 2006–07, 2007–08, 2011–12

COPA DEL REY (19)

1904-05, 1905-06, 1906-07, 1907-08, 1916-17, 1933-34, 1935-36, 1945-46, 1946-47, 1961-62, 1969-70, 1973-74, 1974-75, 1979-80, 1981-82, 1988-89, 1992-93, 2010-11, 2013-14

SPANISH SUPER CUP (9)

1988, 1989, 1990, 1993, 1997, 2001, 2003, 2008, 2012

CHAMPIONS LEAGUE (11)

1955–56, 1956–57, 1957–58, 1958–59, 1959–60, 1965–66, 1997–98, 1999–2000, 2001–02, 2013–14, 2015–16

UEFA CUP (2)

1984–85, 1985–86

UEFA SUPER CUP (2)

2002, 2014

INTERCONTINENTAL CUP (3)

1960, 1998, 2002

FIFA CLUB WORLD CUP (1)

2014

BALLON D'OR

Alfredo di Stefano (1957, 1959)
Raymond Kopa (1958)
Luis Figo (2000)
Ronaldo (2002)
Fabio Cannavaro (2006)

FIFA BALLON D'OR

Cristiano Ronaldo (2013, 2014)

ESTADIO SAN

HONOUR

FIFA WORLD PLAYER OF THE YEAR
Luis Figo (2001)
Ronaldo (2002)
Zinedine Zidane (2003)
Fabio Cannavaro (2006)

UEFA CLUB FOOTBALLER OF THE YEAR
Fernando Redondo (1999-2000)
Zinedine Zidane (2001-02)

UEFA BEST PLAYER IN EUROPE
Cristiano Ronaldo (2013-14)

WORLD SOCCER PLAYER OF THE YEAR
Luis Figo (2000)
Ronaldo (2002)
Cristiano Ronaldo (2013, 2014)

EUROPEAN GOLDEN SHOE
Hugo Sanchez (1989-90)
Cristiano Ronaldo (2010-11, 2013-14, 2014-15)

CHAMPIONS LEAGUE TOP SCORER
Alfredo di Stefano (1957-58)
Ferenc Puskás (1959-60, 1963-64)
Michel (1987-88)
Raul (1999-2000, 2000-01)
Cristiano Ronaldo (2012-13, 2013-14, 2014-15, 2015-16)

LA LIGA TOP SCORER
Manuel Olivares (1932-33)
Pahino (1951-52)
Alfredo di Stefano (1953-54, 1955-56, 1956-57, 1958-59)
Ferenc Puskás (1959-60, 1960-61, 1962-63, 1963-64)
Amancio (1968-69, 1969-70)
Juanito (1983-84)
Hugo Sanchez (1985-86, 1986-87, 1987-88, 1989-90)
Emilio Butragueño (1990-91)
Ivan Zamorano (1994-95)
Raul (1998-99, 2000-01)
Ronaldo (2003-04)
Ruud van Nistelrooy (2006-07)
Cristiano Ronaldo (2010-11, 2013-14, 2014-15)

MEET

Already a hero at the Bernabeu after five brilliant seasons with Los Blancos as a player, Zinedine Zidane became the club's new manager in January 2016 and within six months the Frenchman had steered the side to glory in the final of the Champions League.

When Rafa Benitez parted ways with Real Madrid at the start of 2016, the club already had the perfect replacement waiting in the wings in Zidane. The former midfielder had returned to the club three years earlier to coach the second team and on the same day as Benitez left, Zidane was promoted to the top job and handed a two-and-a-half year deal.

"I'm going to put my heart and soul into this club," he said. "We're the best club in the world, with the best fans in the world. What we have to do, and what I'm going to try to do, is make every possible effort to see this team win something this season. I'm going to work as hard as I can and to the best of my ability with all the players and I believe that everything will turn out well." (realmadrid.com)

THE MANAGER

The team were already safely through to the knockout stages of the Champions League when he was appointed but it was Zidane who masterminded their unstoppable march to the final with victories over Roma, Wolfsburg and Manchester City in the semi-final.

The final took Los Blancos to Italy to face city rivals Atletico Madrid in Milan. It went all the way to penalties and it was Zidane's players who held their nerve in the shootout to beat Atletico 5-4 for the club's record-breaking 11th European triumph.

In the process Zidane became the first French manager to lift the trophy, the seventh man to win the Champions League as a player and then as manager and only the eighth coach to claim European football's greatest prize in his first season in the dugout.

'Zizou' was already a favourite with the Madrid faithful but he had now become a true legend.

The Zidane story began in 1989 when he signed for French side Cannes as a teenager. He spent seven years in France before a big money move to Juventus in Italy. But it was when he arrived at the Bernabeu in 2001 for a then world record fee of £46.6million that he became a global star.

Blessed with outrageous skills, power, technique and incredible vision, the attacking midfielder was an instant hit in Madrid and although he would spend only five seasons at the Bernabeu, he still made 225 appearances for the club and scored 49 goals.

His most influential season as the Real playmaker came in 2002-03 as Los Blancos were crowned La Liga champions. During his time in Spain, he was also a key part of the side which won the Champions League in 2002, two Super Cups and the Intercontinental Cup.

The final of the Champions League against Bayer Leverkusen in Glasgow provided the most iconic moment of his Madrid career, the Frenchman famously scoring the winner with a breathtaking left-footed volley from the edge of the area to seal a ninth European title for Los Blancos. It was a strike which also earned him the Man of the Match award.

Zizou was just as brilliant at international level for France. He won 108 caps for Les Bleus and scored two goals against Brazil in the final of the World Cup in 1998, once again winning the Man of the Match award. He was also in the French side which won the European Championship two years later after beating Italy 2-1 in extra time in the final.

Unsurprisingly Zidane won a huge haul of individual awards while he was a player at the Bernabeu. In 2002 he was named the UEFA Club Footballer of the Year and 12 months later he was the FIFA World Player of the Year. In 2004 he was the winner of the UEFA Golden Jubilee Poll to find the best European footballer of the last 50 years. Zizou received an incredible 123,582 votes in the poll.

He kicked off his managerial career with Madrid with a 5-0 thrashing of Deportivo La Coruna in La Liga in January and in his first six games in charge Los Blancos hit the net 23 times. His first El Clasico against Barcelona as manager came in April at the Nou Camp and ended in a famous 2-1 victory for the club. In total, Zidane was in the hot seat for 27 matches in his first season, the team recording 21 wins in Spain and Europe and finishing on the losing side just twice.

His greatest moment was of course the final of the Champions League against Atletico. The match came 14 years after Zizou had lifted the trophy with Madrid as a player and although he was not out on the pitch pulling the strings in 2016, Zidane was once again at the heart of another famous European night for the club.

MEET THE MANAGER

THE SANTIAGO
IN NUMBERS

EVERYTHING HOME OF

70 GOALS SCORED BY LOS BLANCOS IN LA LIGA IN 2015-16 – THE MOST SCORED AT HOME BY ANY CLUB IN THE DIVISION.

81,044 MATCHDAY CAPACITY OF THE GROUND.

45 HEIGHT IN METRES OF THE TALLEST SECTION OF THE STADIUM.

1944 YEAR THE CLUB BEGAN BUILDING THE BERNABEU IN MADRID ON THE SITE OF ITS OLD GROUND, THE CAMPO DE CHAMARTÍN.

19 CHAMPIONS LEAGUE GOALS SCORED BY LOS BLANCOS AT THE BERNABEU IN 2015-16.

68 WIDTH OF THE BERNABEU PITCH IN METRES. IT IS 105 METRES LONG.

10 GOALS SCORED IN DECEMBER AT THE BERNABEU BY MADRID IN THE LEAGUE AGAINST RAYO VALLECANO - THE TEAM'S BIGGEST VICTORY OF THE SEASON.

330,089 TOTAL ATTENDANCE FOR THE FOUR FIXTURES THE STADIUM STAGED DURING THE 1982 FIFA WORLD CUP.

33 GOALS NETTED BY CRISTIANO RONALDO AT THE GROUND IN 2015-16 IN ALL COMPETITIONS.

4 EUROPEAN CUP FINALS THE GROUND HAS HOSTED. LOS BLANCOS BEAT FIORENTINA 2-0 AT HOME IN 1957 WHILE THE STADIUM ALSO STAGED THE FINALS IN 1969, 1980 AND 2010.

BERNABEU

YOU NEED TO KNOW ABOUT THE LEGENDARY LOS BLANCOS.

2007 YEAR IN WHICH MADRID PLAYED THEIR 1000TH MATCH AT THE BERNABEU – A LEAGUE MATCH AGAINST LEVANTE.

4 FOUR GAMES HOSTED AT THE GROUND DURING THE 1982 FIFA WORLD CUP, INCLUDING THE FINAL BETWEEN WEST GERMANY AND ITALY.

1955 YEAR IN WHICH THE CLUB OFFICIALLY CHANGED THE NAME OF THE STADIUM FROM THE ESTADIO CHAMARTIN TO THE SANTIAGO BERNABEU IN HONOUR OF THE MADRID PRESIDENT.

11 GOALS MADRID SCORED AT THE GROUND AGAINST ELCHE IN 1960. THE 11-2 WIN IS STILL THE CLUB'S RECORD VICTORY IN LA LIGA.

68,929 THE CLUB'S AVERAGE ATTENDANCE IN LA LIGA DURING 2015-16.

2 GOALS SPAIN SCORED AGAINST THE SOVIET UNION AT THE BERNABEU IN 1964 TO WIN THE FINAL OF THE EUROPEAN CHAMPIONSHIPS.

1997 YEAR IN WHICH THE BERNABEU BECAME AN ALL-SEATER STADIUM.

80,148 CROWD FOR THE EL CLASICO CLASH WITH BARCELONA IN NOVEMBER 2015.

124,000 RECORD ATTENDANCE AT THE STADIUM WHEN LOS BLANCOS PLAYED FIORENTINA IN 1957.

2008 YEAR IN WHICH MIDFIELDER GUTI SCORED FOR MADRID AGAINST NUMANCIA AT THE BERNABEU, THE CLUB'S 5000TH GOAL IN LA LIGA.

1957 YEAR IN WHICH LOS BLANCOS PLAYED THEIR FIRST-EVER GAME UNDER FLOODLIGHTS AT THE GROUND.

RONALDO

"What Ronaldo does you cannot name, it is on another historic level. It is incredible what he has done, scoring an average of more than 50 goals a season, when it used to be hard for me to reach 20."
- RAUL (espnfc.co.uk)

"If Messi is the best on the planet, Ronaldo is the best in the universe. Probably the best ever. I saw Maradona a couple of times. I never saw Pele. But Cristiano is amazing. This man is the best, he is a goals machine, an incredible player. He is like Zidane, there will never be another Ronaldo."
- JOSE MOURINHO (independent.co.uk)

"What can I say about Cristiano Ronaldo? He has showed again he is the best player in the world. He is a special player."
- ZINEDINE ZIDANE (goal.com)

"One day I will tell my son, 'once upon a time there was Cristiano Ronaldo'. It's a fairy tale."
- IKER CASILLAS (twitter.com/rmadridfact)

"He's the most ambitious player I've met, with the hunger he has in each game and the desire to score in each match. His winning mentality, his desire, and his ambition to always want more make him a player who's making history in football."
- XABI ALONSO (thenational.ae)

"The next time you compare Ronaldo with another player, take a nap, you're not well."
- RAFAEL NADAL (quora.com)

IN QUOTES

"He is one of the best players ever, the best forward in the history of football. I have never coached a better player than him. Ronaldo is a unique player for all of his talent and his professionalism. He is a player who is extraordinary."
   - CARLO ANCELOTTI (goal.com)

"I have nothing but praise for him. He is easily the best player in the world. His contribution as a goal threat is unbelievable. His stats are incredible. Strikes at goal, attempts on goal, raids into the penalty box, headers. It is all there. Absolutely astounding."
   - SIR ALEX FERGUSON (espnfc.co.uk)

"The numbers speak for themselves. Someone who scores so many goals deserves a place in history. There is no doubt about that. He deserves his place just like Raul and Alfredo Di Stefano. We are talking about three historic players here."
   - RAFA BENITEZ (goal.com)

"Comparing Ronaldo and Messi is like comparing an alien with a human. Ronaldo doesn't have blood. He's perfect."
   - PEPE (quora.com)

"I fear none in the track. Maybe if Ferrari Ronaldo comes in the track, I may tremble."
   - USAIN BOLT (yahoo.com)

RONALDO ON RONALDO

"I am a very private person and I am down-to-earth. My family comes first and my son is the most important thing in my life. I salute him in the crowd every time I score a goal. After that it's the football that matters most to me. Money comes after that."
(mirror.co.uk)

"All around the world I have to deal with my fame. I can't go anywhere without being recognised, which can be very hard."
(thesun.co.uk)

"I am not a perfectionist but I like to feel that things are done well. More important than that, I feel an endless need to learn, to improve, to evolve, not only to please the coach and the fans, but also to feel satisfied with myself. It is my conviction that there are no limits to learning, and that it can never stop, no matter what our age."
(ronaldo7.net)

GARETH BALE

The Flying Welshman was in brilliant form during the 2015-16 season, as he helped Los Blancos lift the Champions League trophy for the second time in his Real career.

It did not take Gareth Bale long to make an impact on Madrid in his third season at the Bernabeu. The world record £85million signing kicked off with two brilliant goals in a 5-0 thrashing of Real Betis in August in the team's second La Liga fixture. The winger never looked back.

In December he was on target four times in a single match as Los Blancos destroyed Rayo Vallecano in Madrid and three weeks later he was in unstoppable form again, hitting a superb hat-trick in the 5-0 demolition of Deportivo La Coruna in Zinedine Zidane's first game as the club's new manager.

His second strike in that victory took his career tally for the club to 50, reaching the half century milestone in only 108 appearances. By the end of the season he had taken his total to 58 goals in just 123 games.

In total Bale scored 19 times in 23 appearances in La Liga, his highest haul in the league since leaving England, and it was the third season in a row he'd reached double figures for the club. He also provided 10 assists for his team-mates during the season.

Bale had already won four major trophies with Los Blancos since signing from Spurs in the summer of 2013 but 2016 was the year he made it five as Madrid were crowned European champions for a record-breaking 11th time.

The Welshman didn't score in the Champions League in 2015-16 but his pace, power and attacking threat were crucial to Madrid reaching the final and, not for the first time, he was the player who created a goal when it really mattered, his glancing first-half header setting up captain Sergio Ramos for Real's opener in the final against Atletico Madrid.

HEROES

Bale then showed his class in the dramatic penalty shootout in Milan that followed, calmly stepping up to take his side's third spot kick and coolly sending the Atletico goalkeeper the wrong way with a beautifully disguised shot.

His first trophy success came in April 2014 when Real faced arch-rivals Barcelona in the final of the Copa del Rey. The game was level at 1-1 with five minutes to play when Bale made his mark with a sensational solo winner, sprinting his own half and outpacing the helpless defence.

He scored again the next month as Los Blancos were crowned champions of Europe. The Champions League final against Atletico Madrid went to extra-time but it was brilliant Bale who put Real ahead with a back post header as Madrid stormed to a famous 4-1 win.

In August Real beat Seville in the UEFA Super Cup to give Bale a trophy treble but by the end of 2104 it was four winner's medals for the flying winger as the team were crowned world club champions.

Bale was sensational in the FIFA Club World Cup, held in Morocco in December 2014, scoring in the 4-1 semi-final victory over Mexican side Cruz Azul and he found the back of the net again in the final as Los Blancos beat Argentinean opponents San Lorenzo 2-0 to finish the tournament as joint top scorer.

LUKA MODRIC

The creative Croatian is the player who pulls the strings in midfield for Los Blancos and has been a star performer for the club since signing from Tottenham Hotspur in 2012.

The 2015-16 season was Luka Modric's fourth for Real Madrid and the talented playmaker was in brilliant form again for the club as Zinedine Zidane's team won the Champions League for a record-breaking 11th time.

Modric may have only scored three times in 44 games for Los Blancos in all competitions but he carved out countless chances for his team-mates and whenever the midfielder had the ball at his feet, Real looked dangerous.

His superb performances for Madrid in Spain and in Europe were a key part of the club's success and at the end of the campaign, Modric was named in both the La Liga and the Champions League Team of the Season for 2015-16.

He began his professional career with Dinamo Zagreb in his native Croatia in 2003 and after five years with the side he signed for Premier League team Tottenham Hotspur in a £16.5 million deal.

In England Modric developed into a world class player. He made over 150 appearances for Spurs, helping the London club reach the quarter-finals of the Champions League in 2011, and was voted the Player of the Season in 2010-11.

Los Blancos beat Tottenham in that quarter-final tie but Real had seen enough of the player to make a bid to sign him and in the summer of 2012 he was on his way to Spain after Spurs accepted £30 million for his signature.

HEROES

In first season at the Bernabeu, the midfielder helped Madrid win the Spanish Super Cup after beating El Clasico rivals Barcelona over two legs and the following season he was in the team that beat Barcelona again in the final of the Copa del Rey in Valencia.

The best was yet to come from the Croatian however and he played a massive part in Real's famous triumph in the 2014 Champions League final against city rivals Atletico Madrid in Lisbon.

Real were 1-0 down in the game in second-half injury time but Modric saved the day with a perfect corner which Sergio Ramos headed home to equalise and send the match into extra-time. Madrid eventually won 4-1 to become European champions for a 10th time.

His great form in 2013-14 was recognised when he was voted La Liga's best midfielder and two months later he celebrated in style as Madrid beat Seville in the UEFA Super Cup in Cardiff. In 2015 Modric was named in the FIFA World XI alongside Bernabeu team-mates Sergio Ramos, Marcelo and Cristiano Ronaldo.

The 2015-16 season was another excellent year for the player. In January 2016 he made his 100th La Liga appearance for the club against Valencia at the Mestalla and in May he added to his impressive collection of winner's medals after Madrid beat Atletico Madrid on penalties in the Champions League final.

In November 2014 Modric signed a new contract with Los Blancos that will keep him at the Bernabeu until 2018, good news for Real fans who have come to worship the brilliant midfielder.

EL CLASICO

The biggest game in Spanish football, matches between Real Madrid and arch-rivals Barcelona have been attracting sell-out crowds for more than 100 years and today are watched by millions on television across the world.

When it comes to sporting rivalries, it doesn't get any bigger than El Clasico and the game between La Liga's two most successful sides. Nearly a billion people tuned in to watch the clubs' two league meetings in 2015-16 and the atmosphere at the Bernabeu when Barcelona are in town is always amazing.

It all started back in 1902 when the teams met in a friendly in Madrid and ever since that first fixture the rivals have been locked in a fierce battle for trophies and titles.

The first competitive meeting of the duo was in 1916 when they were drawn against each other in the semi-finals of the Copa del Rey but the rivalry reached new heights in 1929 when La Liga was formed and what has become an annual battle to be crowned Spanish champions began.

That first league match saw Los Blancos beat Barca 2-1 at their old Camp de Les Corts stadium and in the early days of the fixture, Madrid were dominant and were beaten just four times in the first 20 league meetings.

EL CLASICO IN NUMBERS

390 Goals in all competitions scored by Real against their El Clasico rivals.

33 Players who've represented both clubs during their career.

16 Goals scored by Cristiano Ronaldo in El Clasico.

231 Matches in all competitions between the two clubs by the end of 2015-16. Los Blancos had 93 wins to Barcelona's 90, with 48 draws.

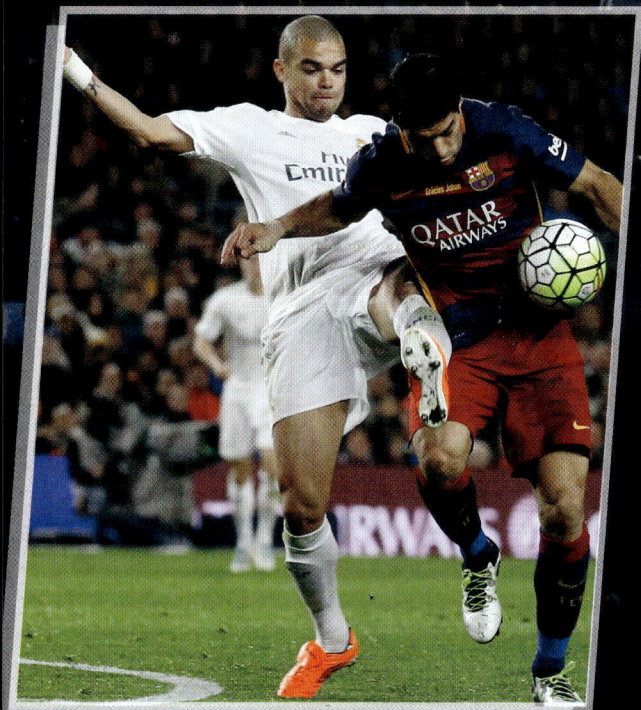

The world famous fixture has produced some classic matches over the years. Madrid's biggest win is their 11-1 defeat of Barca in a cup match back in 1943 while one of Real's most important recent victories against their old rivals came in 2012 when Cristiano Ronaldo scored a late winner away at the Nou Camp to secure a 2-1 success, a result which helped Los Blancos seal the championship.

Such is the massive popularity of the match that in 2010 a film was released called 'El Clasico: More Than A Game', an hour-long documentary shot in the two biggest cities in Spain looking at the long and explosive history of the fixture.

The 2015-16 season saw Barcelona win at the Bernabeu in November but Zinedine Zidane's side got their revenge in April with a 2-1 victory at the Nou Camp thanks to goals from Cristiano Ronaldo and Karim Benzema.

El Clasico has also seen the old rivals meet eight times in the Champions League over the years and Madrid are in front in the European head-to-head with three wins to Barcelona's two.

EL CLASICO IN NUMBERS

172 League meetings between the two clubs since the first La Liga clash in 1929.

72 Madrid league victories over Barca in the famous fixture.

280 League goals scored by Los Blancos against Barcelona.

10 Goals scored by Madrid in their record 11-1 win against Barca in the Copa del Rey in 1943.

*Stats correct at end of 2015-16 season.

CRISTIANO RONALDO TRIVIA

HERE IS THE LOWDOWN ON REAL MADRID'S GLOBAL SUPERSTAR.

Ronaldo has worn Nike boots throughout his career. Since 2010 he has played in a series of specially designed boots, including the Superfly II Safari CR7, while in 2014 he switched to the new Mercurial Superfly CR7.

In December 2013 the Portuguese forward opened a museum called 'Museu CR7' in his hometown of Funchal on the island of Madeira to display the trophies and memorabilia from his football career.

According to a study, Ronaldo was the top earning sportsman in the world in 2015. The striker earned a cool £61 million to overtake boxer Floyd Mayweather Junior in the rich list, £38.5 million coming from his salary at Real Madrid and the rest from his sponsorship deals with companies like Nike and exclusive watchmaker Tag Heuer.

He published his autobiography called 'Moments' in December 2007 while a documentary film about his life and career called 'Ronaldo' was released

at cinemas worldwide in November 2015. Ronaldo has lent his name to a series of video games including Pro Evolution Soccer 2008, Pro Evolution Soccer 2012 and Pro Evolution Soccer 2013.

The star was the first ever sportsman to reach 50 million followers on Facebook in August 2010. By June 2015 he had an incredible 103 million followers. He is also the most popular athlete on Twitter with 37.8 million followers by September 2015.

At the age of 15, Ronaldo was diagnosed with a serious heart condition and had to undergo surgery to cure the problem and allow his football career to continue.

In June 2010 Ronaldo became only the fourth ever footballer to have a waxwork of himself unveiled at the world famous Madame Tussauds in London. The other players are Brazil legend Pelé, Steven Gerrard and his former Manchester United team-mate David Beckham.

In 2015 a group of astronomers discovered a new galaxy and named it CR7 in tribute to the Bernabeu icon.

Since he began his professional career at Sporting Lisbon back in 2002, clubs have spent a massive £92.24 million on transfer fees for Ronaldo.

When Ronaldo signed for Los Blancos in 2009, the club sold an incredible 1.2 million replica shirts in the nine months after he arrived in Spain, generating £80 million in sales. A crowd of 80,000 packed the Bernabeu just to watch his official unveiling.

In November 2012 he put the European Golden Shoe award he had won for scoring 50 goals for Real in 2010-11 up for auction. It sold for £1.2 million which he donated to a children's charity.

Ronaldo does not have any tattoos because he regularly gives blood and any body ink would mean he would not be allowed to donate.

QUIZ TIME

FIND OUT HOW BIG A REAL MADRID FAN YOU ARE WITH OUR BRILLIANT QUIZ. ALL THE ANSWERS CAN BE FOUND SOMEWHERE IN THIS ANNUAL.

1. GARETH BALE PLAYS INTERNATIONAL FOOTBALL FOR WHICH COUNTRY?

2. IN WHAT YEAR DID ZINEDINE ZIDANE SCORE THE WINNING GOAL IN THE FINAL OF THE CHAMPIONS LEAGUE AGAINST BAYER LEVERKUSEN?

3. FROM WHICH CLUB DID LOS BLANCOS SIGN CAPTAIN SERGIO RAMOS IN 2005?

4. HOW MANY GOALS IN ALL COMPETITIONS DID CRISTIANO RONALDO SCORE DURING THE 2015-16 SEASON?

5. HOW MANY TIMES HAVE MADRID BEEN CROWNED EUROPEAN CHAMPIONS?

6. CRISTIANO RONALDO AND WHICH OTHER PLAYER SCORED THE GOALS IN REAL'S 2-1 VICTORY OVER BARCELONA AT THE NOU CAMP IN EL CLASICO IN APRIL 2016?

7. WHO SCORED THE WINNING PENALTY IN THE SHOOTOUT IN THE CHAMPIONS LEAGUE FINAL AGAINST ATLETICO MADRID IN MILAN?

8. LUKA MODRIC JOINED LOS BLANCOS FROM WHICH ENGLISH TEAM IN 2012?

9. IN WHAT YEAR WAS THE FIRST EVER EL CLASICO BETWEEN REAL AND BARCELONA?

10. MADRID BEAT MANCHESTER CITY 1-0 ON AGGREGATE IN THE CHAMPIONS LEAGUE SEMI-FINALS. WHO SCORED THE GOAL?

11. WHAT BRAND OF BOOT DOES CRISTIANO RONALDO WEAR?

12. HOW MANY GAMES WERE PLAYED AT THE BERNABEU DURING THE 1982 WORLD CUP FINALS?

13. GARETH BALE SCORED HIS 50TH GOAL FOR THE CLUB IN 2015-16 AGAINST WHICH CLUB?

14. BERNABEU DEFENDER PEPE WAS BORN IN WHICH COUNTRY?

15. LOS BLANCOS PLAYED WHICH TEAM IN THEIR FIRST GROUP GAME OF THE 2015-16 CHAMPIONS LEAGUE CAMPAIGN?

16. WHO DID ZINEDINE ZIDANE REPLACE AS MANAGER IN JANUARY 2016?

17. HOW MANY TIMES HAS SERGIO RAMOS WON LA LIGA SINCE SIGNING FOR LOS BLANCOS?

18. LUCAS VAZQUEZ, GARETH BALE, SERGIO RAMOS, CRISTIANO RONALDO AND WHICH OTHER PLAYER WERE ALL ON TARGET FOR REAL IN THE CHAMPIONS LEAGUE PENALTY SHOOTOUT?

19. HOW MANY LA LIGA SEASONS IN A ROW HAS CRISTIANO RONALDO NOW SCORED OVER 30 GOALS IN?

20. DEFENDER NACHO SCORED HIS ONLY GOAL IN 2015-16 IN THE CHAMPIONS LEAGUE AGAINST WHICH TEAM?

21. HOW MANY LEAGUE GOALS DID REAL SCORE AT THE BERNABEU IN THE 2015-16 SEASON?

22. CAN YOU NAME THE COUNTRY MATEO KOVACIC PLAYS INTERNATIONAL FOOTBALL FOR?

23. HOW MANY LA LIGA GAMES DID MADRID LOSE IN 2015-16 WITH ZINEDINE ZIDANE AS MANAGER?

24. WHICH TEAM DID LOS BLANCOS FACE IN THE 2015-16 CHAMPIONS LEAGUE QUARTER-FINALS?

25. WHAT AWARD DID CRISTIANO RONALDO AUCTION IN 2012 TO RAISE MONEY FOR CHARITY?

26. IS THE MATCHDAY CAPACITY OF THE BERNABEU 78,346 OR 81,044?

27. IN WHAT YEAR DID THE SANTIAGO BERNABEU BECOME AN ALL-SEATER STADIUM?

28. HOW MANY TIMES HAVE THE SPANISH GIANTS WON THE INTERCONTINENTAL CUP?

29. FROM WHICH ITALIAN SIDE DID THE CLUB SIGN ZINEDINE ZIDANE IN 2001?

30. WHO SCORED THE REAL GOAL IN THE FIRST HALF OF THE CHAMPIONS LEAGUE FINAL AGAINST ATLETICO MADRID IN 2016?

Answers on p.60-61

TRUE OR FALSE?

CAN YOU TELL FACT FROM FICTION WITH THESE REAL MADRID TEASERS?

1. ☐ ▶ Real Madrid have never been relegated from La Liga.
2. ☐ ▶ Madrid manager Zinedine Zidane was born in the French city of Marseille.
3. ☐ ▶ The Bernabeu is the biggest stadium in Spain.
4. ☐ ▶ As a teenager Cristiano Ronaldo had surgery to cure a heart problem.
5. ☐ ▶ Los Blancos signed Gareth Bale from Arsenal in 2013.
6. ☐ ▶ Madrid have won La Liga a record-breaking 32 times.
7. ☐ ▶ Madrid faced Bayern Munich in the final of the 2016 Champions League.
8. ☐ ▶ Sergio Ramos replaced Iker Casillas as club captain in 2015.
9. ☐ ▶ Goalkeeper Keylor Navas made the most appearances for Real during the 2015-16 season.
10. ☐ ▶ Los Blancos have won the Champions League 10 times.
11. ☐ ▶ Cristiano Ronaldo is the captain of Spain.
12. ☐ ▶ Los Blancos were sponsored by airline Fly Emirates in 2015-16.
13. ☐ ▶ The Santiago Bernabeu was opened in 1957.
14. ☐ ▶ Pepe was the team's vice captain in the 2015-16 season.
15. ☐ ▶ Toni Kroos was a World Cup winner with Germany in 2014.

Answers on p.60-61

WORDSEARCH

```
A O S A V A N F K T R Y E
R A H R K R O O S C O J P
B M V C L R V P A C D O E
E E Q M A A T S I J L L P
L Z V M C N E R M Z A E C
O N Z I T M D E E R N C A
A E C R I O N U K D O R S
R B L R M A Q D B C R A I
A D O Q R Z W H A A N M L
M Y R A A W R J E N L T L
O V V V R V C Z B S I E A
S R O D R I G U E Z E L D
T W L A J A V R A C Z J O
```

ARBELOA
BALE
BENZEMA
CARVAJAL
CASEMIRO
CASILLA
DANILO
JESE
KOVACIC
KROOS

MARCELO
MODRIC
NACHO
NAVAS
PEPE
RAMOS
RODRIGUEZ
RONALDO
VARANE
VAZQUEZ

Answers on p.60-61

QUIZ ANSWERS

Quiz Time (p56-57)

1. Wales
2. 2002
3. Seville
4. 51
5. 11
6. Karim Benzema
7. Cristiano Ronaldo
8. Tottenham Hotspur
9. 1902
10. Gareth Bale
11. Nike
12. Four
13. Deportivo La Coruna
14. Portugal
15. Shakhtar Donetsk
16. Rafa Benitez
17. Three
18. Marcelo
19. Six
20. PSG
21. 70
22. Croatia
23. One
24. Wolfsburg
25. European Golden Shoe
26. 81,044
27. 1997
28. Three
29. Juventus
30. Sergio Ramos

True or False? (p58)

1. True
2. True
3. False
4. True
5. False
6. True
7. False
8. True
9. True
10. False
11. False
12. True
13. False
14. False
15. True

Word search (p59)

```
A O S A V A N F K T R Y E
R A H R K R O O S C O J P
B M V C L R V P A C D O E
E E Q M A A T S I J L L P
L Z V M C N E R M Z A E C
O N Z I T M D E E R N C A
A E C R I O N U K D O R S
R B L R M A Q D B C R A I
A D O Q R Z W H A A N M L
M Y R A A W R J E N L T L
O V V V R V C Z B S I E A
S R O D R I G U E Z E L D
T W L A J A V R A C Z J O
```